Holiday 2 Explorer

English for short courses

HEINLE
CENGAGE Learning™

Australia • Brazil • Japan • Korea • Mexico • Singapore • Spain • United Kingdom • United States

Welcome to Holiday Explorer!

This book will help you to learn, practise and remember English … and it's easy to use!

You will find the following in each of the 6 units:

- *Vocabulary* an entertaining introduction to new words
- *Dialogue* language in interesting situations
- *Grammar* lots of revision and practice
- *Functions* useful language for the daily lives of young people
- *Skills* practise new language and learn about culture
- *Wizard!* a fun magazine just for you

Remember!
- Whenever you see this symbol  use the audio CD.
- Turn to the grammar reference section at the back of the book when you need extra help.
- Complete the word list at the back of the book and remember all the words you learn.

CRACK THE CODE

Each unit finishes with a code cracking activity. Solve the puzzles and find hidden words.

So, what are you waiting for?

Contents

Shopping

Vocabulary

① Look and match

Look at the things to buy in the box. Write them in the correct shops in the street plan.

carrots	aspirin	bread	meat	apples	cakes
newspaper	flowers	flight	chicken	toothbrush	TV guide

NEWSAGENT'S   BUTCHER'S   CHEMIST'S   BAKER'S   GREENGROCER'S   TRAVEL AGENTS   Florist's

HIGH STREET

② Unscramble

Read the clues and unscramble the names of these shops.

1   You buy flowers in this shop.

   o l i t s f r 's _____

2   You buy a holiday here.

   e r l v t a   g a t n e 's _____

3   This is where you buy medicine.

   h t i m c s e 's _____

4   You buy fruit and vegetables here.

   e c o r r g r e n g e 's _____

③ Write

Look at these shops. Write two things you can buy in each shop.

1   newsagent's _____

2   greengrocer's _____

3   baker's _____

4   chemist's _____

5   butcher's _____

④ Listen and read

Listen to this conversation and follow it in your book.

Mum   Come on. Let's go to the new Woodside Shopping Centre.

Alice   Great idea! The best shops are there.

Brian   Oh, Mum, I like shopping but I hate shopping with you and Alice.

Mum   But you want some new trainers.

Brian   Well, yes I do, but I like buying trainers from the sports shop in town.

Alice   I love shopping. Why don't you and I go to Woodside Shopping Centre together, Mum?

Mum   No, I need to see what Brian wants before I pay for them.

Alice   Well, I don't mind shopping with you, but the shops at Woodside are better than the shops in town.

Mum   Yes, and they are also bigger and cheaper than the ones in town!

Brian   OK! But what about buying my trainers first, then I can go and do what I want. I hear that the biggest computer games shop in the country is there. Come on. Let's go!

⑤ Comprehension

Read the dialogue again. Tick (✓) the correct sentences.

1   Mum wants to take Alice and Brian to the shops in town. ◯

2   Brian wants some new trainers. ◯

3   Mum needs to see the trainers that Brian wants. ◯

4   Alice hates shopping with Brian. ◯

5   Alice prefers the shops in town. ◯

6   Brian wants to buy his trainers first. ◯

⑥ Find the sentence

Look at the word grid. A word is hidden in every line. Read all the words and you will find a sentence. What is the sentence?

B	B	R	I	A	N	N	N	G	J	K
R	T	Y	U	D	O	E	S	N	T	L
G	L	I	K	E	A	A	S	D	F	J
O	M	T	S	H	O	P	P	I	N	G
Q	X	W	I	T	H	E	B	N	M	K
F	R	I	S	A	L	I	C	E	F	G

Grammar

Verbs followed by the -ing form

1 **Put the words in the box into the sentences below.**

hate
don't like
~~love~~
doesn't mind
like

 1 I ____love____ buying flowers.

2 She _____ playing tennis.

3 I _____ shopping with my brother.

 4 Do you _____ reading the newspaper?

5 We _____ going to the doctor's.

2 **Look at the pictures and write the sentences.**

1   Katie / like / swim
Katie likes swimming.

2   Michael / not like / do the washing up
_____

3   Sally and Janet / enjoy / sing
_____

4 Peter / not mind / do his homework
_____

3 **Comparatives and superlatives**
Complete the table.

	adjective	comparative	superlative
regular	tall	taller	the tallest
	big	1 _____	the biggest
	young	2 _____	3 _____
	old	4 _____	5 _____
	easy	easier	6 _____
	cheap	7 _____	8 _____
	expensive	9 _____ expensive	10 the most _____
	difficult	11 _____	12 _____
	boring	13 _____	14 _____
irregular	good	better	15 _____
	bad	16 _____	the worst
	fun	17 _____ fun	18 _____

Need help? Go to page 52!

④ Look at the pictures and complete the sentences using the comparative form of the adjectives.

| tall | bad | fun | expensive | good | difficult |

1   Jim is _____ *taller* _____ than Rick.

2   Maths is _____ than music.

3   Football is _____ than homework.

4   The weather in Italy is _____ than the weather in Britain.

5   Hamburgers are _____ for us than salad.

6   A Ferrari is _____ than a Fiat.

⑤ Read the table and complete the sentences using superlatives.

	age	weight	height	school marks	swimming records	sprint records 100 m
Chris	12	35 kg	120 cm	good	50 lengths per hour	13.15
Alan	15	40 kg	150 cm	very good	30 lengths per hour	12.02
Carla	13	41 kg	140 cm	not very good	40 lengths per hour	14.16

1   Chris is 12. He is (young) _____ *the youngest* _____ .

2   Alan is 15. He is (old) _____ .

3   Carla weighs 41 kg. She's (heavy) _____ .

4   Chris is 120 cm tall. He's (short) _____ .

5   Carla's marks are not very good. She's (bad) _____ student.

6   Alan's marks are very good. He's (intelligent) _____ student.

7   Chris swims 50 lengths per hour. He's (good) _____ swimmer.

8   Alan runs 100 metres in 12.02. He's the (fast) _____ runner.

Functions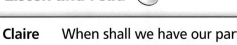

Offering, making suggestions and making excuses

① Listen and read

Claire	When shall we have our party?
John	Well, your birthday's on the sixth, mine's on the tenth and Linda's is on the twelfth, so why don't we have it on Saturday the eighth?
Linda	OK, great! Where shall we have it?
John	Shall we have it at your house, Linda? You've got the biggest garden.
Linda	But my house isn't big and my mum is very busy. What about your place?
John	No, I'm sorry. We can't have it at my house because dad's boss is at our house for dinner on the eighth.
Claire	Let's have it at my house, then. My mum loves parties.
John	Really? That's cool.
Linda	Why don't we go to your house after school today, Claire, and ask your mum if it's OK?
Claire	Good idea.

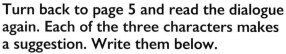

② Comprehension

Read the dialogue again. Tick (✓) the true sentences below. Correct the false sentences.

1 The three friends are planning a birthday party. _____
_____

2 Claire's birthday is on the fifth.
_____
_____

3 Linda has got the biggest garden. _____
_____

4 Claire's mum hates parties. _____
_____

5 They decide to have the party at Linda's house. _____
_____

③ Read and think

Draw a wavy line under the offers in the dialogue, draw a straight line under the suggestions and circle the excuses.

④ Look and write

Turn back to page 5 and read the dialogue again. Each of the three characters makes a suggestion. Write them below.

1 Mum: let's _____

2 Alice: _____

3 Brian: _____

⑤ Reorder

Reorder the words to make sentences. Which sentence is an excuse (E), which is an offer (O), and which is a suggestion (S)?

1 about / what / after / cinema / the / going / to / the / school? _____
_____

2 me / with / help / let / you / that.
_____

3 can't / party / I / go / I'm / the / to / because / busy. _____
_____

Skills

① Read

Read this article about shopping. What can you buy in a shopping centre?

We all love shopping for fun now!

The Institute of International Research tells us that Europe is now a continent of shoppers. People love going shopping just for the fun of it. It isn't only the rich who do this now – it's all of us! We have more money than before and these shopping centres and malls offer lots of things to see, do and buy!

Today people have busy lives and at weekends they enjoy spending much more time shopping in one place. Families now love going shopping together. Shopping isn't only about buying the food for the week. Now there are big changes, and everyone wants to spend their free time walking around the big shopping centres and malls. The shops in these large modern shopping centres and malls are cheaper than the smaller shops in the towns so they are the best places for families to buy clothes, books, and the latest computer games. It's a perfect day out!

② Comprehension

Read the article again and answer these questions.

1 Where do many European families spend more of their free time now?

_____

2 Why do families enjoy going to these large shopping centres and malls? Underline the reasons in the text.

③ Listen

Listen to the woman talking about shopping and answer the questions.

1 What shops does she mention in the village?

_____

2 Where does she go for her clothes and things for the house?

_____

3 Why doesn't she like shopping in the town?

_____

4 How is she different from the people in the reading article?

_____

WORD LIST

mall _____

busy life _____

day out _____

④ Write

Write about your attitude to shopping. Think about these things:

✓ Do you enjoy shopping? Why? / Why not?

✓ Where and when do you go shopping? (town centre / mall / hypermarket?)

✓ Who do you go shopping with?

✓ What are your favourite shops?

Shopping and me!

The Grand Canyon

Read the text. What is the opposite of each word in bold?

1 _____
2 _____
3 _____

The Grand Canyon is very ¹ **old**! It's about six billion years old! About four million people visit it every year.

Some people think the Grand Canyon is in Nevada because it's not very far from Las Vegas. It is in Arizona.

The Grand Canyon is fantastic! A very ² **long** river, the Colorado River, created it many years ago.

The Grand Canyon is incredible. It is very deep. One part of the canyon is 1.6 kilometres deep. You can go down into the deepest part of the canyon by mule! It is exciting but sometimes it is a bit scary! It is very long too – 446 kilometres long. That is a long walk!

It is also really ³ **beautiful**. The layers of rock you can see have lots of colours!

WORD LIST

a bit scary _____
create _____
deep _____
down _____
layer _____
mule _____
rock _____
walk _____

② Comprehension

Read the text on page 10 again and then do the quiz on the Grand Canyon. Tick (✓) the correct answers.

1 Where is the Grand Canyon?

   a Colorado

   b Nevada

   c Arizona

2 What created the Grand Canyon?

   a a river

   b ice

   c people

3 The deepest part of the canyon is ____ deep.

   a 10 kilometres

   b 1.6 kilometres

   c 500 metres

4 You can see layers of ____ as you go down into the Grand Canyon.

   a rock

   b cake

   c glass

③ Write

Complete the sentences with the superlative form of the words in the box.

long	wide	tall	high

1 The Amazon is the _____ river in the world.

2 Everest is the _____ mountain in the world.

3 Angel Falls is the _____ waterfall in the world.

4 The Nile is the _____ river in the world.

WOW!

The Colorado River, which flows through the Grand Canyon, is almost 2330 km long, ending in Mexico. The name is Spanish and it means 'red'.

CRACK THE CODE

④ Find the words. Which word is the odd one out?

1 tnoumnia _____

2 irrve _____

3 twrllaaef _____

4 ncaeo _____

5 kcor _____

6 llvaye _____

The odd one out is: _____

2

Vocabulary

① Read and complete

Joe lives in England. He is going to Florence for a holiday. Write the means of transport Joe takes under each picture.

by train	by bus	on foot	by plane	by taxi
by tube	by car	by bicycle (bike)	on a scooter
by motorbike	by tram	by boat

┌─────────────────┐   ┌─────────────────┐
│ Joe goes …   │   │ Joe doesn't go … │
└─────────────────┘   └─────────────────┘

1 *on foot*   4 _____   7 _____   10 _____

2 _____   5 _____   8 _____   11 _____

3 _____   6 _____   9 _____   12 _____

Can I go to Florence?

2 Listen and read ⌕⁴

Listen to the dialogue and follow it in your book.

Tommy	Mum, can I ask you something?
Mum	Yes. What is it?
Tommy	Well, I was at Joe's house yesterday, and he had a holiday with his dad in Italy last month.
Mum	That's nice. Where?
Tommy	They were in Florence and they had a really nice time.
Mum	Florence – how lovely! Did they have fun?
Tommy	Yes, they did, but Joe didn't have a friend with him, so he wants me to go with him next time. Can I go with him in July?
Mum	I'm sorry, but you can't. We are on holiday in July.
Tommy	Well, is it OK if I go in August, then?
Mum	No, not really. It's probably too expensive.
Tommy	Mum, the flight and hotel are both really cheap. Joe flies to Florence and then goes by bus and taxi to the hotel. Is it all right if I use my birthday money to pay for it?
Mum	Well, OK. Sure!
Tommy	Thanks, Mum!

3 Comprehension

Read the dialogue again. Decide if these sentences are true (T) or false (F). Correct the false sentences.

1 Tommy was at Joe's house yesterday._____

_____

2 Mum doesn't like Florence. _____

_____

3 Joe had a bad time in Florence. _____

_____

4 Mum says Tommy can go in July. _____

_____

5 The flight and hotel aren't cheap. _____

_____

4 Find the sentence

Find the hidden word in each line of the grid to make a sentence.

Q	T	O	M	M	Y	J	P	D
W	A	N	T	S	A	H	U	I
B	E	U	S	J	L	M	T	O
W	G	O	G	J	I	U	Y	W
X	C	S	T	O	Y	T	R	V
Y	F	L	O	R	E	N	C	E

Write the sentence here:

_____

_____

Grammar

The verb *be* (past simple)

① Complete the table.

affirmative	negative	question	short answer
I / he / she / it / *was*	I / he / she / it 1 _____	2 _____ I / he / she / it?	Yes, I / he / she / it 3 _____ . No, I / he / she / it 4 _____ .
you / we / they 5 _____	you / we / they 6 _____	7 _____ you / we / they?	Yes, you / we / they 8 _____ . Yes, you / we / they 9 _____ .

② Put the time phrases in the box into the correct chronological order.

> ~~last month~~   the day before yesterday   today   two weeks ago   yesterday   three days ago

1 _____*last month*_____   3 _____   5 _____

2 _____   4 _____   6 _____

③ Look at the pictures and complete the sentences.

1   Last summer Carl and his family __*were*__ on holiday in Greece – the weather _____ beautiful.

2   Stephanie _____ late – her teacher _____ happy.

3   There _____ 1,000 passengers on the boat – they _____ all very excited.

4   There _____ lots of people on the bus and they _____ very angry.

5   The passengers _____ bored because their flight _____ an hour late.

6   Nick _____ happy with the result but Richard _____ .

Need help? Go to page 53!

The verb *have* (past simple)

④ **Complete the table.**

affirmative	negative	question	short answer
I / he / she / it / you / we / they	I / he / she / it / you / we / they	Did I / he / she / it / you / we / they	Yes, I / he / she / it / you / we / they
1 _____	2 _____	3 _____ ?	4 _____ .
			No, I / he / she / it / you / we / they
			5 _____ .

⑤ **Look at the pictures and complete the sentences with the correct past simple form of *have*.**

1   When I was four I _____*had*_____ a tricycle.

3   We _____ any tickets for the concert.

2   She _____ her passport.

4   '_____ the Romans _____ cars?' 'No, they _____ .'

⑥ **Complete the postcard with the correct past simple form of the verbs *be* and *have*.**

Hi Sandra,
1 ___*Did*___ you ___*have*___ a nice time in England?
Our holiday in Greece 2 _____ fantastic.
The weather 3 _____ great, sunny and warm.
The beaches 4 _____ a bit busy but they
5 _____ beautiful. We 6 _____ the chance
to visit Athens, but next time I really want
to go there!
What about London? I hope the weather
7 _____ too bad! 8 _____ you _____
the time to go to Cambridge?

See you soon,
Simon

Hi from Greece!

Need help? Go to page 53!

Functions

Asking for permission
Giving and refusing permission

① **Listen and read** 🔘⁵

Jane	Hello, Mum. I'm home.
Mandy / Paul	Hello, Mrs Jones.
Mrs Jones	Come in. Let's have a cup of tea.
Jane	Thanks, Mum. Can we ask you something? We had an idea today. We want to have a party together for our three birthdays next month. Could we have it here?
Mandy	I can't have a party at my house.
Paul	And my parents are busy that day.
Mrs Jones	Well, when do you want to have it?
Paul	Is it OK if we have it on the eighth?
Mrs Jones	I'm afraid that's not possible – it's Grandpa's birthday that day.
Jane	What about the fifteenth then?
Mrs Jones	Yes, sure. That's fine.
Jane	Oh, thanks, Mum!

② **Comprehension**

Read these sentences and tick (✓) the correct ones.

1. a ⬤ Mrs Jones is Jane's mother.
   b ⬤ Mrs Jones is Mandy and Paul's mother.

2. a ⬤ They want to have a party at Mandy's house.
   b ⬤ They want to have a party at Jane's house.

3. a ⬤ Paul's parents want the party at their house.
   b ⬤ Paul's parents are busy that day.

4. a ⬤ The party is on the eighth.
   b ⬤ The party is on the fifteenth.

③ **Read and think**

Read the dialogue on page 13 again and the dialogue on this page.

✓ Circle the permission requests in both dialogues.

✓ Draw a straight line where permission has been refused

✓ Draw a wavy line where permission has been given.

④ **Make requests**

Read the sentences below and write a request for each one.

1 Ask your mum to give you £15 for a CD.

_____

2 Ask your dad if he can help you with your English homework.

_____

3 Ask your neighbour, Mr Smith, if he can drive you to the station.

_____

Skills

① Read

Read the article about Elvis Presley. Name some things that Elvis liked.

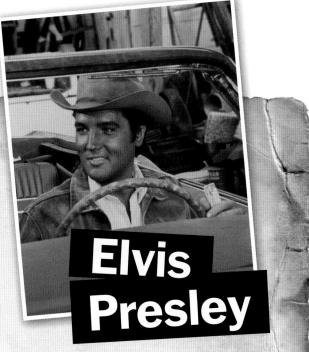

Elvis Presley

Elvis Presley was an American singer and actor. He was born in Tupelo, a town in the South of the USA, on 8th January 1935. His parents weren't very rich and for many years they had a very simple life.

Elvis was married to Priscilla Presley. They had one daughter, Lisa Marie, but they didn't have any sons.

In the 1950s, 60s and 70s Elvis was very successful and had lots of hit songs, for example Jailhouse Rock, Hound Dog and Blue Suede Shoes.

Elvis liked many different types of transport: aeroplanes, motorcycles and cars. His favourite aeroplane was very big and its name was The Lisa Marie. It had a bedroom, a bathroom, an office and even a bar! There were also four TVs and a huge music system. Elvis's biggest passion was cars, and in particular Cadillacs. In his life he had more than 100! His favourite Cadillac was pink and white and was a present for his mother, Gladys. It is probably one of the most famous cars in the world!

② Comprehension

Read the article again and decide whether these sentences are true (T) or false (F). Correct the false sentences.

1   Elvis's parents were very rich. _____

_____

2   Elvis and Prescilla had two daughters. _____

_____

3   Elvis had a very big aeroplane, called The Lisa Marie. _____

_____

③ Write

Write some sentences about your favourite type of transport. Use these questions to help you.

✓   What is your favourite type of transport?

✓   What colour is it?

✓   When do you use it?

④ Listen and answer 🔘⁶

Listen to the questions about Paula and her family and write the answers.

1   Who is talking? Tick (✓) the correct answer.

   a   Paula and her friend Mike _____

   b   Paula and her father _____

   c   Paula and her mother _____

2   Complete the sentence.
    Paula wants to go to the _____ next _____ evening in Newcastle.

3   Paula asks if she can use the car. Write what she says.

   a   _____

   b   _____

4   She wants to go the concert next Sunday with

   a   her father. _____

   b   her boyfriend. _____

MOUNT ETNA

① Read

Read the text and find all the adjectives.

I am a photographer and I love volcanoes. I am lucky because I am from Sicily and I live near Catania. Mount Etna is a fantastic volcano and it is active. This is a photograph of it and we were very close to it! The lava was about 1700 degrees Fahrenheit and we were only a few metres away. It was very dangerous. The lava was so hot!

Sometimes it was hard to breathe because there wasn't a lot of air and there was a lot of poisonous gas.

Eruptions are fantastic but it is always a dangerous experience. But, I love my job!

There are a lot of volcanoes in the world and I often go and see them.

WORD LIST	
away	_____
poisonous	_____
lucky	_____
breathe	_____
eruptions	_____
dangerous	_____

② Read the text on page 18 again and answer the questions.

1   What is the man's job?

   _____

2   Where is he from?

   _____

3   Where is Mount Etna?

   _____

4   How hot is the lava?

   _____

5   Why are volcanoes dangerous?

   _____

6   Can you think of some other volcanoes in the world?

   _____

WOW!

There are at least 1,500 active volcanoes in the world. Indonesia is the country which has the most volcanoes.

CRACK THE CODE

③ The biggest volcano in the world is Mauna Loa. It's found in the U.S.A. on an island. Find out where it is by looking at the letters in the river of lava.

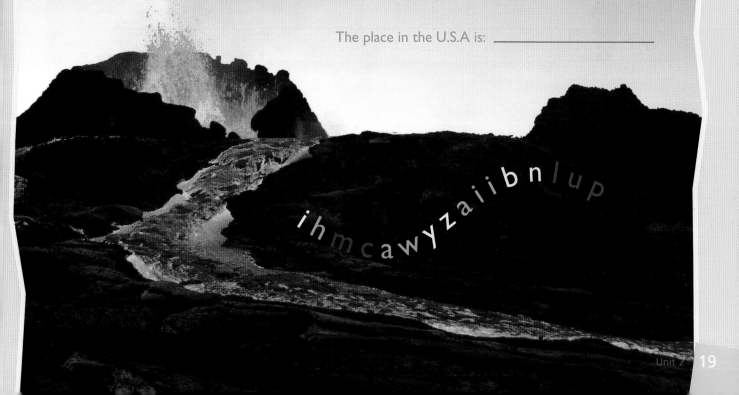

The place in the U.S.A is: _____

i h m c a w y z a i i b n l u p

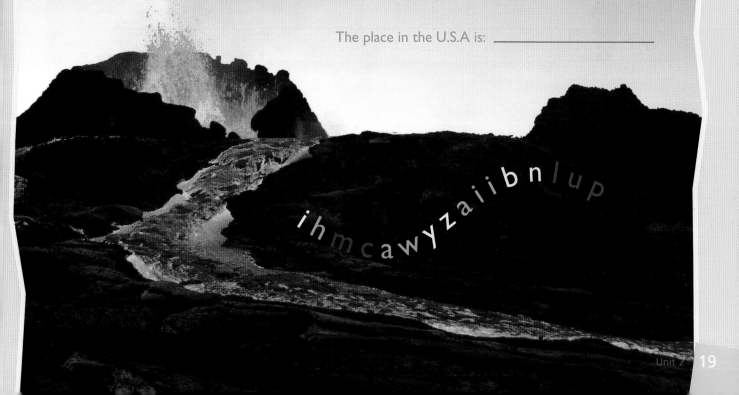

Vocabulary

1 Complete the crossword

Complete the crossword with the party and celebration words in the box. Use the pictures to help you.

| birthday | sleepover | New Year | pool | wedding | Halloween | Christmas | fancy dress |

Across

Down

1 F A N C Y D R E S S

2 Write

Write the dates for:

1 New Year _____

2 Your birthday _____

3 The start of the summer holiday _____

4 The end of the summer holiday _____

3 Choose

Circle the correct words in these sentences.

1 It's a beautiful day! Let's have a **pool party** / **a sleepover**.

2 I want to wear my pirate costume to the **fancy dress party** / **wedding**.

3 I'm 18 next week, please come to my **birthday** / **New Year** party!

What a party!

Listen to the dialogue and follow it in your book.

Kirstie That was a good party last night. Did you like it, Julie?

Julie Yes, it was great! I love fancy dress parties.

Danny Me too! Your costume was good, Julie. Did you design it?

Julie No, I didn't. My mum designed it. It started as an angel costume and finished up as a fairy!

Danny Well, you looked fantastic!

Julie Thanks! And you looked really good in your costume, too, Danny.

Danny I watched Pirates of the Caribbean again last week, and I wanted to be a pirate at the party!

Julie Did you like Peter's costume?

Kirstie Yeah – his cowboy costume was great! He was the best of the boys, and I think you were the best of the girls, Julie.

Danny I agree about Peter – it wasn't an expensive costume but it looked really good.

Julie Well, I think you were the best of the girls, Kirstie – you were a beautiful princess.

Danny A 'beautiful princess'?

Kirstie Danny!

5 Comprehension

Answer the questions.

1 Who went to the fancy dress party?

_____

2 Who was a fairy at the party?

_____

3 Who watched a film about pirates?

_____

4 Which boy had the best costume?

_____

5 Who was a princess?

_____

6 Read and match

Match the things on the left to the type of party on the right.

Things		Party
1	cake with candles	a	New Year
2	pyjamas	b	Halloween
3	swimming costume	c	sleepover
4	champagne at midnight	d	fancy dress
5	witches and ghosts	e	birthday
6	interesting costumes	f	pool

Grammar

The past simple (regular verbs)

① Complete the table.

affirmative	negative
I _wash_	I _didn't wash_
you [1] _____	you [2] _____
he / she / it [3] _____	he / she / it [4] _____
we _washed_	we [5] _____
you [6] _____	you [7] _____
they [8] _____	they _didn't wash_

② Form the simple past of these regular verbs.

infinitive	past simple
stop	[1] _____
invite	[2] _____
start	[3] _____
cry	[4] _____
play	[5] _____
organise	[6] _____
stay	[7] _____
study	[8] _____
travel	[9] _____
shop	[10] _____
celebrate	[11] _____

③ Complete the sentences with some of the verbs from Exercise 2.

1 Last Saturday was Mum's birthday and we _____organised_____ a surprise party for her.

2 Last summer I _____ to the USA – it was amazing!

3 The fancy dress party _____ at 8 o'clock.

4 Frank _____ New Year last year – he was too tired.

5 I _____ Nicole to my sleepover because I don't like her.

④ Complete the table.

question	short answer
___Did___ I _wash_ ?	Yes, you ___did___ . / No, you _didn't_ .
[1] _____ you _____ ?	[2] Yes, I _____ . / No, I _____ .
Did he / she / it _wash_?	[3] Yes, he / she / it _____ . / No, he / she / it _____ .
[4] _____ we _____ ?	[5] Yes, we _____ . / No, we _____ .
[6] _____ you _____ ?	Yes, you ___did___ . / No, you _didn't_ .
[7] _____ they _____ ?	[8] Yes, they _____ . / No, they _____ .

⑤ Write past simple questions and short answers in the affirmative (+) and negative (–).

1 the party / finish / late? (+)
   Did the party finish late?
   Yes, it did.

2 You / watch / DVDs / at the sleepover? (–)
   _____
   _____

3 James / cry / after the exam? (–)
   _____
   _____

4 they / stay / at a 5-star hotel? (+)
   _____
   _____

5 Duncan / celebrate / his birthday / last week? (–)
   _____
   _____

Need help? Go to page 54!

6 Write questions for the answers below using the question words in the box.

~~What~~   Why   What time
Where   How many

1 _____ *What did you celebrate* _____?

I celebrated my birthday.

2 _____?

The party was in our big garden.

3 _____?

We invited about 15 people.

4 _____?

I cried because I was very happy.

5 _____?

The party finished at 5 o'clock.

7 Complete email with the correct past simple form of the verbs.

To: robert@mymail.com
From: kate.williams@teenmail.co.uk
Subject: Hi Robert!

Hi Robert,

How are you?

I'm very well, I ¹_____ (want) to write to you and tell you about my trip to London last weekend. It ²_____ (be) great!

We ³_____ (travel) from Birmingham to London by train on Friday and ⁴_____ (stay) in a lovely hotel next to the London Eye.

On the first day we ⁵_____ (visit) all the famous sights in London: Big Ben, the Houses of Parliament, Covent Garden and then in the afternoon we ⁶_____ (shop) on Oxford Street.

The next day we ⁷_____ (want) to go to the theatre. We ⁸_____ (hope) to find tickets to the musical *Hairspray*, and we did! I ⁹_____ (love) the show and at the end everybody ¹⁰_____ (dance) to the music. I ¹¹_____ (have) a fantastic time!

On the last day we ¹²_____ (plan) to go to the British Museum in the evening, but we ¹³_____ (be) too late! It ¹⁴_____ (close) at 5.30 p.m. and we ¹⁵_____ (arrive) at 6 p.m.!

So that's my news, write to me soon and tell me yours!

Kate

Functions

Inviting someone to do something
Accepting and declining

① Listen and read 🄸⁸

Angela Shall we invite some friends from the youth club to a party?

Tracy Good idea. Who do you want to invite?

David Let's invite Emily Parks. She's nice.

Tracy Yes, I like her too. Let's phone and ask her. …
Hi, Emily. It's Tracy.

Emily Hello, Tracy.

Tracy David, Angela and I are having a party. Would you like to come?

Emily Wow! That's great! Thanks very much. I'd really like to come. When is it?

Tracy It's on Saturday.

Emily OK. I need to check with my mum, then I can tell you tomorrow.

Tracy Great! Speak to you tomorrow!

② Comprehension
Read the dialogue again. Tick (✓) the true sentences below. Correct the false sentences.

1 Angela wants to invite some friends from the football team to the party._____
_____

2 David wants to invite Emily to the party.
_____
_____

3 Tracy doesn't like Emily. _____
_____

4 Emily doesn't want to come to the party.
_____
_____

③ Read and find
Find examples of the following things in the dialogue:

1 Two suggestions:
   a _Shall we_____? b _____

2 Inviting someone:
   _____

3 Giving a reply:
   _____

4 Two exclamations:
   a _____! b _____!

④ Reorder
Reorder the words to make sentences. Which two sentences are invitations (I)? Which two sentences accept an invitation (A), and which two decline an invitation (R)?

1 to / like / I'd / really / go. _____
_____

2 can't / I'm / go / I / the / to / I'm / afraid / because / party / busy. _____
_____

3 party / come / would / next / you / to / my / like / to / week? _____
_____

4 want / go / do / to / you / to / cinema / on / the / Saturday? _____
_____

5 can't / I'm / go / I / but / the / to / I'm / sorry / because / cinema / busy. _____
_____

6 I'd / to / love / thanks, / come. _____
_____

Skills

① Listen and read 🔟⁹

Listen and circle the correct answer.

1 What was Jane's best party?
   a Her sister's New Year's Eve party.
   b An old school friend's party.
   c Her sister's birthday party.

2 Where was the party?
   a In a hotel in town.
   b In a hotel in the country.
   c In a beautiful garden.

3 The party finished at …
   a two o'clock in the morning.
   b two o'clock in the afternoon.
   c three o'clock in the morning.

4 Jane didn't …
   a dance to a band.
   b stay the night at the hotel.
   c travel back to London on a coach.

② Read and answer

Read the article below then complete the sentences.

What makes a good party?

A friend invited me to a big party at a very expensive hotel in Italy, last year. The hotel was beautiful. It was a large hotel with a lovely garden, and was next to a private lake. The weather was sunny and warm, and the food and drink were delicious. The party lasted five hours, from midday until five o'clock in the afternoon. But it wasn't a good party.

I realised that the problem was the people who were at the party. They didn't know each other and had very different lifestyles. They didn't mix, they didn't talk, and they weren't interested in each other. So I decided that a successful party is not really about the place and the food and the drinks, but it's about the people you invite. You have to invite lots of people who know and like each other, but who are also ready to enjoy meeting some new and interesting people.

1 The author says that a bad party is one where _____
_____ .

2 A good party is one where _____
_____ .

③ Write

Write about a good party you went to. Think about these questions:

✓ Whose party was it?
✓ Where and when was it?
✓ What was the food and drink like?
✓ Who was there?
✓ How long did it last?

Example:

Last year I was invited to a party.
It was my cousin's party and
_____

Niagara Falls

Complete the postcard with the correct form of the past simple.

Dear Antonio

I am in New York! It is fantastic! We ¹ **arrive** _____ this morning. My family and I ² **travel** _____ here by car. It ³ **is** _____ a long journey but we all ⁴ **enjoy** _____ it. Yesterday we ⁵ **are** _____ in Canada, at Niagara Falls! It ⁶ **is** _____ amazing. We ⁷ **stay** _____ at a hotel near the famous waterfalls. We ⁸ **watch** _____ fireworks in the evening. My sister, Francesca ⁹ **likes** _____ the fireworks but I ¹⁰ **prefer** _____ the helicopter tour! It ¹¹ **is** _____ great!

New York is lots of fun!

See you soon

Ben

Fact file

Interesting facts about Niagara Falls

- Some of it is in Canada and some of it is in the United States.
- There are three different falls, American Falls, Bridal Veil Falls and Horseshoe Falls.
- The Niagara River is a young river, only 12,000 years old!
- The Falls are about 55 metres high.
- These are the second largest falls in the world.
- 20 per cent of the world's fresh water is in the Great Lakes and comes over Niagara Falls.
- 12 million people visit the falls every year.
- Superman was filmed at the falls.

WORD LIST

fireworks	_____	helicopter tour	_____
fresh water	_____	waterfalls	_____
fun	_____	horseshoe	_____

② Comprehension

Read the postcard on page 26 again and correct the sentences.

1 The Niagara Falls are in Mexico.

   _____

2 40 per cent of the world's fresh water is in the Great Lakes.

   _____

3 Niagara Falls is the largest waterfall in the world.

   _____

4 There are two different falls there.

   _____

> **WILD!**
>
> Some people believe that the word 'Niagara' comes from the native American word "onguiaahra", meaning "thundering water", but others believe it to mean "the strait".

③ Write

Complete these sentences with the past simple.

1 Today, we call it the United States.

   In the past, people _____ it the New World.

2 We travel by car today.

   In the past, people _____ by horse and carriage.

3 Today, we watch TV.

   In the past, people _____ plays at the theatre.

CRACK THE CODE

④ Complete the crossword about Niagara Falls. What is the new word?

1 They made this famous film at Niagara Falls.

   __ __ __ __ __ __ __ __

2 The opposite of short. __ __ __ __

3 The __ __ __ __ __ Lakes

4 The past of *do* __ __ __

5 The Niagara Falls are in this country.

   __ __ __ __ __ __

Films

Vocabulary

1 Read and write

Match the film types in the box with the pictures.

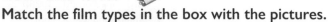

| comedy | horror | thriller | musical | romance |
| science fiction | | historical | action | detective |

1 _____thriller_____

4 _____

7 _____

2 _____

5 _____

8 _____

3 _____

6 _____

9 _____

2 Choose

Read the sentences and circle the correct film genre.

1 I love Jack Black's films. He is very funny and makes me laugh! **action / comedy**

2 These films are usually about space, aliens and other worlds. **horror / science fiction**

3 I love these kinds of films – the actors sing and often dance a lot too. **thriller / musical**

4 My sister loves films where people meet and fall in love. But I think they're boring! **romance / detective**

5 My mum likes watching films about the past, like the Kings and Queens of Britain. **historical / comedy**

What did you do last night?

③ Listen and read

Listen to the dialogue and follow it in your book.

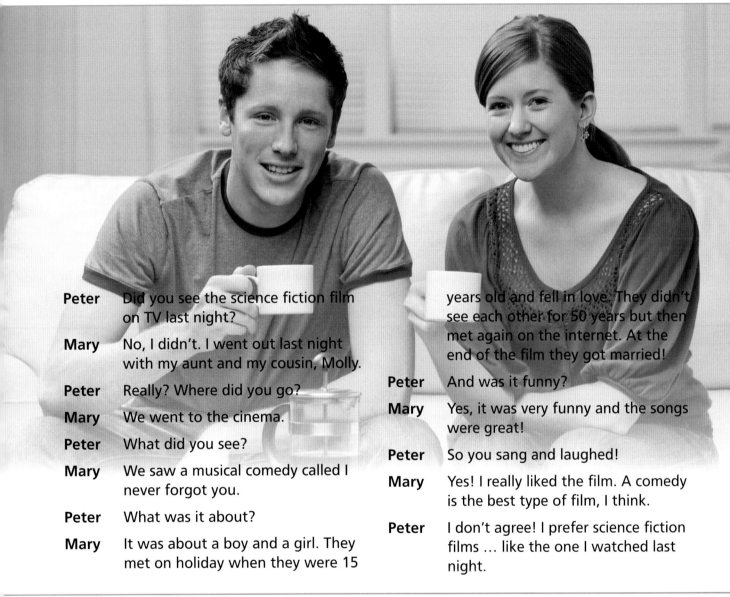

Peter Did you see the science fiction film on TV last night?

Mary No, I didn't. I went out last night with my aunt and my cousin, Molly.

Peter Really? Where did you go?

Mary We went to the cinema.

Peter What did you see?

Mary We saw a musical comedy called I never forgot you.

Peter What was it about?

Mary It was about a boy and a girl. They met on holiday when they were 15 years old and fell in love. They didn't see each other for 50 years but then met again on the internet. At the end of the film they got married!

Peter And was it funny?

Mary Yes, it was very funny and the songs were great!

Peter So you sang and laughed!

Mary Yes! I really liked the film. A comedy is the best type of film, I think.

Peter I don't agree! I prefer science fiction films … like the one I watched last night.

④ Comprehension

Read the dialogue again. Tick (✓) the true sentences below.

1 Mary went to the cinema with her mother and sister. ◯

2 Mary watched a science fiction film last night. ◯

3 The film wasn't very funny. ◯

4 Mary liked the film she saw at the cinema. ◯

5 Peter watched a horror film last night. ◯

⑤ Write

Rewrite the false sentences from exercise 4 here so that they are true.

_____

_____

_____

_____

_____

_____

_____

_____

Grammar

The past simple (irregular verbs)

① Complete the tables.

affirmative	negative
I *gave*	I *didn't give*
you *saw*	you [1] _____
he / she / it [2] _____	he / she / it *didn't do*
we [3] _____	we [4] _____ *come*
you *went*	you [5] _____
they [6] _____	they *didn't sing*

question	short answers
Did I give?	Yes, you *did.* / No, you *didn't.*
Did you see?	Yes, I [7] _____ / No, I [8] _____ .
[9] _____ he / she / it do?	Yes, he / she / it *did.* / No, he / she / it *didn't.*
Did we come?	Yes, we [10] _____ / No, we [11] _____ .
[12] _____ you go?	Yes, you *did.* / No, you *didn't.*
Did they sing?	Yes, they [13] _____ / No, they [14] _____ .

② Put these words into the correct order.

1 well / sleep / yesterday / didn't / very / Helen

   Helen didn't sleep very well yesterday.

2 saw / cinema / we / at / Mr Jones / the

   _____

3 for / they / dinner / did / pay / ?

   _____

4 cost / it / ? / did / what

   _____

5 cake / a / delicious / made / you

   _____

6 to / day / I / every / him / wrote

   _____

③ Complete the table with the bare infinitive or past simple of the verbs.

infinitive	past simple
speak	[1] _____
[2] _____	said
eat	[3] _____
[4] _____	drank
read	[5] _____
[6] _____	wrote
buy	[7] _____
[8] _____	run

④ Find the 16 past simple irregular verbs in this word snake. Indicate each verb with a |.

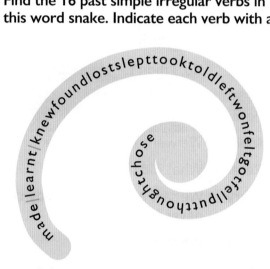

⑤ Match the questions to the answers.

1 What kind of film did you see? d

2 Did Jessica sing in the concert? ◯

3 What time did you get here? ◯

4 Did you buy any milk? ◯

5 What was the film like? ◯

a At 3 o'clock.

b It was great!

c No, I didn't.

d A thriller.

e Yes, she did.

Need help? Go to page 55!

⑥ **Write these sentences in the negative form.**

1 Pete bought the tickets for the film.
   Pete didn't buy the tickets for the film.

2 I ate three packets of popcorn.
   _____

3 Simon saw an interesting thriller.
   _____

4 They slept for 12 hours.
   _____

5 We made cakes for the party.
   _____

6 I found £10 in my jacket pocket.
   _____

⑦ **Write the sentences from exercise 6 in the question form. Then write a positive or negative answer, as shown.**

1 _____
   (+) _____

2 _____
   (–) _____

3 _____
   (–) _____

4 _____
   (+) _____

5 _____
   (+) _____

6 _____
   (–) _____

⑧ **Complete this dialogue with the past simple of the verbs in brackets (some are regular, some are irregular).**

Barbara	What [1] *did you do* (you / do) yesterday afternoon?
Sarah	Nothing much. I [2] _____ (stay) at home and [3] _____ (watch) TV. What about you?
Barbara	I [4] _____ (go) to the cinema with Louise.
Sarah	What [5] _____ (you / see)?
Barbara	A historical film, The Queen of Scotland.
Sarah	[6] _____ (you / like) it?
Barbara	Oh no! It [7] _____ (be) so boring that I [8] _____ (fall) asleep ....
Sarah	Really? I [9] _____ (think) it [10] _____ (be) a good film.
Barbara	No, it [11] _____ (not be). We [12] _____ (leave) after half an hour. We [13] _____ (not know) what to do, so we [14] _____ (go) shopping in town. I [15] _____ (buy) a T-shirt and a bracelet.
Barbara	Well done!

Functions

Agreeing and disagreeing

① Listen and read

Anna	What type of party do you want to have?
Nick	Why don't we have a fancy dress party? I love fancy dress!
Anna	Me too! Let's have a theme … Prince and Princesses or Astronauts … like these! What do you think?
Louise	Sorry, but I don't think it's a good idea. It's very expensive to buy a costume.
Nick	No, it's fine. We can make the costumes!
Anna	Let's do something special!
Louise	Well OK, that's fine with me, but let's have a theme that is easy.
Nick	Yes, I agree. How about a Caribbean theme?
Anna	I think that's a great idea. We can wear colourful clothes and sunglasses!
Louise	Yes, great theme, let's do that!

② Comprehension

Match the parts of the sentences about the dialogue.

1 Nick and Anna both   d
2 Louise doesn't think that
3 Anna likes the idea
4 Nick suggests
5 In the end they all agree that a

a   of a Prince and Princess theme for the party.

b   Caribbean theme for the party is a great idea.

c   a fancy dress party is a good idea.

d   want to have a fancy dress party.

e   that they have a Caribbean theme.

③ Read and find

Read the dialogue again. Underline the places where somebody disagrees and circle the places where they agree.

④ Write

Look at the statements below and agree or disagree with them. If you disagree, give a reason why.

1   I think footballers earn too much money.

_____

2   Formula 1 motor racing is a really interesting sport.

_____

3   I don't think it's important to go to university.

_____

4   It isn't important to learn English.

_____

5   Chemistry is a very easy subject.

_____

6   It's important for famous pop stars and actors to be attractive.

_____

7   Hip-hop music is the best!

_____

8   Romantic films are boring.

_____

Read

**Read the film review and answer the questions.
(Note: we can use the present tense when we are
describing a story – see paragraph two of the review.)**

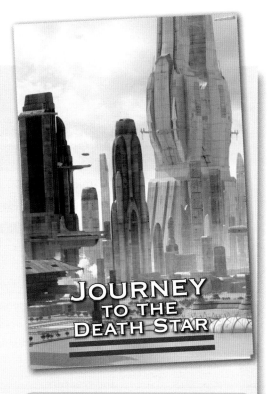

CINEMA NEWS AND VIEWS

Last night I went to the cinema and saw the third film in the *Space
Lord* series, called *Journey to the Death Star*. It was a classic
science fiction film, full of all the usual special effects that we
know and love: space ships, aliens, fights between the good and
bad characters. Daniel Johnson was great as the leader of the
Space Lords, and the new actor, Julie Chan, was also excellent
as Princess Chet.

The story is about a rescue mission. The evil aliens take Princess
Chet on the day of her wedding to the Space Lord. They take
her to the Death Star, which is a prison. The Space Lord does
everything he can to find her. At the end of the film he finds her
and saves her, but only after a series of problems and lots of
explosions! I don't agree with the newspaper reviewers – they
didn't like it but I think it's a really exciting film!

WORD LIST

fights _____

special effects _____

rescue mission _____

1 What type of film is it? _____

2 Who are the actors in the film? _____

3 Where do the aliens take Princess Chet? _____

4 Is the writer positive or negative about the film? _____

② Listen and answer

**Listen to the conversation and answer the
questions.**

1 What are the two people talking about?

   _____

2 What type of film is a Bond film?

   _____

3 What is the name of the horror film Ben
   saw?

   _____

4 Which film do you think Ben liked best?

   _____

5 Does Jackie like horror films?

   _____

③ Write

**Write a review of a film you watched
recently. Write about:**

✓ what type of film it is

✓ who the actors are

✓ the story

✓ what you liked and didn't like about it

Title: _____

_____

_____

_____

THE ANCIENT EGYPTIANS

① Read

Complete the text with the words in the box.

> mummies   pyramids   died
> tomb   papyrus   gold   pharaohs

There are about 140 [1] _____ in Egypt. The largest one is the Great Pyramid at Giza near Cairo.

The Ancient Egyptians created a fantastic civilisation. The [2] _____ were the kings and queens. They had a lot of [3] _____ and treasure.

They used pictures for reading and writing. These were hieroglyphics. They wrote on [4] _____ .

The Ancient Egyptians made [5] _____ . They believed that you went to another life when you died. The pyramids were their tombs.

King Tut was one of the most famous pharaohs. He [6] _____ 3,327 years ago. He was only nineteen years old. An English archaeologist, Howard Carter, found his [7] _____ in the Valley of the Kings in 1922. There was a lot of treasure! There were also a few female pharaohs. The most famous are Nefertiti, Cleopatra and Hatshepsut, who was the first woman to become pharaoh.

King Tut

The Great Pyramid

Hieroglyphics

mummy

WORD LIST

hieroglyphics   _____
treasure   _____

② Comprehension

Read the text on page 34 again and answer the questions.

1   What did the Ancient Egyptians build and use as tombs?

They built pyramids and used them as tombs.

2   How many pyramids are there in Egypt?

_____

3   What did the Ancient Egyptians believe about death?

_____

4   When did King Tut die?

_____

5   Who was the first female pharaoh?

_____

WOW!

The ancient Egyptians didn't believe that the brain was important and they removed it when they made mummies.

③ Write

Complete these sentences with the past simple.

1   Today, Egyptians sometimes eat chicken, lamb and beef.

Ancient Egyptians sometimes

_____ pelicans!

2   Today, Egyptians have olive oil.

Ancient Egyptians _____ sesame oil.

CRACK THE CODE

④ Unscramble the words. Can you find the word for another ancient civilisation?

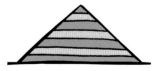

1   ymumm

_____

2   hopraah

_____

3   diyprma

_____

The ancient civilisation is: _____

Vocabulary

① Read and complete

Read the descriptions and write the names in the correct place on the map.

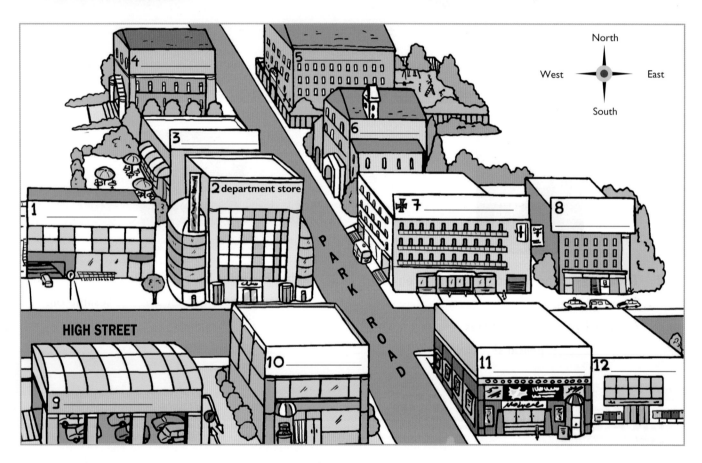

- The **department store** is on the corner on the north side of the High Street and the west side of Park Road.

- The **supermarket** is next to the department store, in the High Street.

- The **café** is next to the department Store in Park Road.

- The **town hall** is next to the café.

- The **bank** is on the corner opposite the department store on the south side of the High Street.

- The **garage** is next to the bank in the High Street.

- The **cinema** is on the corner opposite the bank on the south side of the High Street.

- The **post office** is next to the cinema in the High Street.

- The **hospital** is opposite the cinema on the other corner of the High Street.

- The **police station** is next to the hospital in the High Street.

- The **library** is opposite the café in Park Road and next to the hospital.

- The **school** is opposite the town hall in Park Road.

What do you have to do today?

② Listen and read

Listen to the dialogue and follow it in your book.

Sam Dad, can you help me with my bike, please?

Dad Sorry, not this morning ... I have to go into town.

Sam Oh, Dad! Do you have to go this morning?

Dad Yes, I do! First I must go to the police station.

Sam Why?

Dad I lost my wallet yesterday, so I must report it. Next I have to go to the bank, to order new credit cards.

Sam Then where?

Dad After that I have to buy Mum some printer paper from that computer shop behind the cinema. She must have it this morning.

Sam Oh, when you are near the cinema can you check what films are on this weekend, please!

Dad OK. I have to go past the cinema, because there are some letters to post at the post office opposite. I mustn't forget because they're important letters. Then, finally, I must return some library books.

Sam Then please can you help me this afternoon?

Dad Sure!

③ Read and write

Read the dialogue again. Sam's father has to go to six places. What are they?

1 _____

2 _____

3 _____

4 _____

5 _____

6 _____

④ Think and write

Where you do these things?

1 You buy stamps here.   *post office*

2 You take your car here.   _____

3 This is a good place to watch a film.   _____

4 You go here if you're very ill.   _____

5 You can sleep here.   _____

6 There are a lot of books here.   _____

Grammar

Must / mustn't

① **Circle the correct word.**

1 To express obligation we use *must* **with / without** *to* + the bare infinitive of the verb.

2 You form the third person singular **with / without** *-s*.

3 To express prohibition we use *mustn't* **with / without** *to* + the bare infinitive of the verb.

② **Complete these sentences with *must* or *mustn't*.**

1 Teacher: You _____*must*_____ listen!

3 Mum: You _____ play computer games all day!

2 Man: Sorry, I _____ go.

4 You _____ use your mobile in class!

③ **Look at the signs, then complete the sentences with *must / mustn't* and a verb from the box.**

fish	smoke	take	drink	be	pay

1 We _____ in the lake.

2 We _____ quiet in church.

3 We _____ the water.

4 We _____ photographs in the museum.

5 We _____ '7 to see the show.

TICKETS £7

6 We _____

Need help? Go to page 56!

Have to / don't have to

④ Complete the table.

affirmative				negative			
I	have to			I	don't	[1] _____	
You	[2] _____			You	[3] _____	[4] _____	
He / She / It	[5] _____	go.		He / She / It	[6] _____	[7] _____	go.
We	have to			We	[8] _____	have to	
You	[9] _____			You	[10] _____	[11] _____	
They	[12] _____			They		have to	

question				short answer
Do	I	have to		Yes, you do. / No, you don't.
[13] _____	you	have to		Yes, I do. / No, I don't.
Does	he / she / it	have to	go?	Yes, he / she / it [14] _____ / No, he / she / it [15] _____ .
Do	we	[16] _____ .		Yes, we do. / No, we don't.
[17] _____	you	have to		Yes, you do. / No, you don't.
Do	they	[18] _____ .		Yes, they [19] _____ / No, they [20] _____ .

⑤ Match the rule to the example sentence.

1	Express obligation.	a	We don't have to wear school uniform tomorrow.
2	Express not having any obligation.	b	I have to study for my exams this weekend.
3	Asking if we have any obligation.	c	Do I have to repeat the question?

⑥ Valentina has found a leaflet for an English course and talks about it to her parents. Complete the dialogue with _have to_ in the affirmative, negative and question forms.

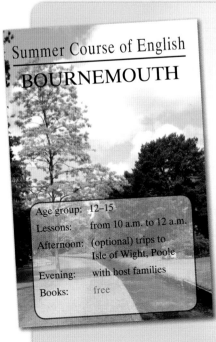

Summer Course of English
BOURNEMOUTH

Age group: 12–15
Lessons: from 10 a.m. to 12 a.m.
Afternoon: (optional) trips to Isle of Wight, Poole
Evening: with host families
Books: free

Valentina Mum, Dad, can I do this English course in Bournemouth this summer?

Mum Let me see ... you [1] _have to_ be from 12 to 15 years old.

Valentina …and I'm 14, so I can go!

Dad OK. How many hours a day [2] _____ you [3] _____ be in school?

Valentina I [4] _____ study English at least three hours a day. But in the afternoon there are trips to the Isle of Wight ....

Dad But those are optional – you [5] _____ go if you don't want to.

Valentina Yes, but I want to see those places!

Mum Well, that sounds great! [6] _____ we [7] _____ pay for the books?

Valentina No, we [8] _____ . They're free.

Need help? Go to page 56!

Functions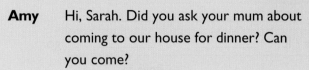

Giving directions

① **Listen and read** 🔘¹⁴

Amy	Hi, Sarah. Did you ask your mum about coming to our house for dinner? Can you come?
Sarah	Yes, I can! What's the best way to your house? I live near the supermarket.
Amy	OK, well, go along the High Street, past the library, and then turn right at the crossroads, after the town hall.
Mike	I think you mean left, Amy!
Amy	Oh, yes, I do – sorry!
Mike	OK, I'll give Sarah directions! Turn left at the crossroads into Palace Street, and go straight on. Go past the school and then turn left, into King's Road. Amy's house is number 27, behind the Swan Hotel.
Sarah	Great, I know where that is. Thanks!

② **Comprehension**

Tick (✓) the correct option.

1 Sarah
   a ⬤ can go to Amy's house for dinner.
   b ⬤ can't go to Amy's house for dinner.

2 Sarah
   a ⬤ knows where Amy lives.
   b ⬤ doesn't know where Amy lives.

3 When she goes to Amy's house Sarah must
   a ⬤ turn right at the crossroads.
   b ⬤ turn left at the crossroads.

4 The school is
   a ⬤ in Palace Street.
   b ⬤ in King's Road.

5 Amy lives
   a ⬤ behind a hotel.
   b ⬤ next to a shop.

③ **Reorder**

Reorder the sentences.

1 the / the / tell / me / way / can / to / you / cinema?

_____

_____

2 give / you / directions / the / me / can / to / library?

_____

_____

3 the / past / straight / on / go / school

_____

_____

4 at / turn / the / crossroads / right

_____

_____

5 the / house / behind / is / my / hotel

_____

_____

6 is / supermarket / the / the High Street / on

_____

_____

Skills

① Read

Read the article and circle the sentences in the text that describe the duties of good citizens.

City life

We all have responsibilities when we live in towns and cities. We must always respect the other people who live near us. We can do this in many small ways, every day. So, what exactly do we have to do to make sure our towns are great places to live? Here are some tips!

1 We mustn't drop rubbish in the street or in our parks. In some cities the police can make you pay if they see you do that. We can make the job easier for the cleaners if we put rubbish into the bins.

2 It is important to make sure that our dogs don't make the streets and parks dirty.

3 We have to think about others and not make too much noise. Loud music, for example, disturbs other people.

4 If we drive a car, we must park it correctly. We mustn't block entrances and pavements. This makes life difficult for others – and they can get very angry!

Let's make our cities and towns happy and safe places to live!

WORD LIST

rubbish	_____
noise	_____
block (v)	_____
disturb (v)	_____

② Listen

Listen to the dialogue and answer the questions.

1 What does Andy have to do this afternoon?

_____

2 What does Lizzie have to do in the afternoon?

_____

3 Where does Andy suggest they go for lunch?

_____

4 What do they agree to do tomorrow?

_____

③ Write

Write about your school rules. Use the following questions to help you.

✓ What time do you have to be at school in the mornings?

✓ Do you have to wear a school uniform?

✓ Can you use mobile phones in class?

✓ Can you talk to friends when the teacher is speaking?

✓ Do you have to go to school on Saturdays?

....

....

....

Polar bears

① **Read**

Read and complete the text with the words in the box.

| don't have to | can't | must | go | need | live |

Polar bears only [1] _____ in the Arctic. They don't live in the Antarctic as some people think. The Arctic is a very cold place but polar bears love it!

They are fantastic animals. They are enormous and can be three metres tall. They are the largest bears on earth. They eat a lot of fish and also seals. They sometimes hibernate and when they hibernate, they [2] _____ to eat for months. They are excellent swimmers and can swim over a hundred kilometres if they want to find food.

Polar bears [3] _____ ice to survive. They [4] _____ hungry without the ice because there aren't enough fish and seals and the baby polar bears (they are called cubs) [5] _____ survive. The ice is melting so they are in danger.

We [6] _____ help to save polar bears. We have to look after our Earth!

WORD LIST

cubs	_____	melt	_____
hibernate	_____	survive	_____
look after	_____	seals	_____

② Comprehension

Read the text on page 42 again and then write below what polar bears *must* and *mustn't* do. Use the expressions in the box.

| eat for months | live in icy places | eat lots of fish and seals | swim a lot |

Polar bears have to

_____

_____

_____

Polar bears don't have to

_____

_____

_____

WOW!

Polar bears don't drink water!

CRACK THE CODE

③ Do the crossword about polar bears.

1 Polar bears eat these.

2 Where we live and it is in danger.

3 Baby polar bears.

4 Polar bears live in the North ___ ___ ___ ___ .

5 Polar bears cannot survive without this.

6 The opposite of hot

What is the new word? _____

Music

Vocabulary

① Read and complete

Complete the crossword. Use the pictures and the words in the box to help you.

saxophone   singer   piano   violin   trombone

clarinet   trumpet   drums   keyboard   guitar   organ

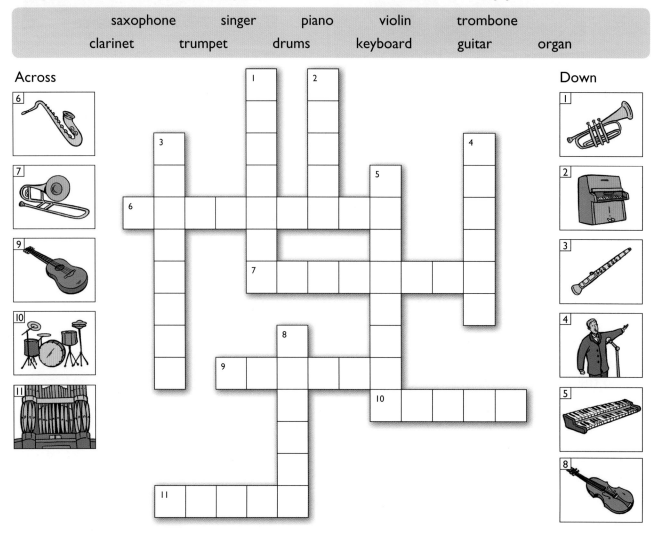

Across

Down

② Choose

Complete the sentences with the correct words.

1 Dad loves listening to **classical** / **pop** music. His favourite composer is Mozart.

2 I prefer traditional **techno** / **folk** music.

3 My brother listens to lots of **rap** / **soul** music. His favourite singer is 50 Cent.

4 I love dancing to **disco** / **classical** music.

5 I'm learning the guitar so I can play my favourite **rock** / **hip-hop** songs.

6 My sister plays the saxophone and she loves playing lots of **electronic** / **jazz** music.

I'm playing in a concert

3 Listen and read

Listen to the dialogue and follow it in your book.

Rock music

Tuesday 5/8 at 8.00.p.m
Underground Club in Park Road

Toby	Hey, I'm going to see a band tomorrow night. Would you like to come with me?
Wendy	I'm afraid I can't. I'm playing in a concert of my own tomorrow.
Toby	Really? What type of concert?
Wendy	I play in a rock band called The Tall Trees.
Toby	I didn't know that. What do you play?
Wendy	I play bass guitar and I'm also the lead singer. Then we have Sam on keyboards, Jenny on drums and Freddie on lead guitar.
Toby	That's great. Where are you playing tomorrow?
Wendy	We're playing at the Underground Club in Park Road.
Toby	What? You're going to be there at eight o'clock tomorrow night?
Wendy	Yes, that's right. Why?
Toby	Because that's where I'm going! I have two tickets from a friend, but it doesn't say what band's playing, just where and when.
Wendy	So you're coming to see us? That's wonderful!
Toby	I'm looking forward to it!

4 Comprehension

Read the dialogue again and match the parts of the sentences below.

1 Toby is going to a ⓑ

2 Wendy sings and plays in ◯

3 The band is ◯

4 Toby is ◯

a coming to hear Wendy's band.

b concert tomorrow evening.

c playing at the Underground Club.

d a rock band with Sam, Jenny and Freddie.

5 Write

Unscramble the letters to make names of musical instruments.

1 n p a o i __ __ __ __ __

2 e a o n h p x s o

__ __ __ __ __ __ __ __

3 t c e a i l n r

__ __ __ __ __ __ __ __

4 i l o v n i __ __ __ __ __ __

5 m u r s d __ __ __ __ __

6 m r t p t u e __ __ __ __ __ __ __

7 n a o r g __ __ __ __ __

8 r i t u g a __ __ __ __ __ __

Grammar

The future with *going to*

① Complete the tables.

affirmative		
I *am* ('*m*)		
you ¹ _____ ('*re*)		
he / she / it *is* ² (_____)	going to	play.
we ³ _____ ('*re*)		
you *are* ⁴ (_____)		
they ⁵ _____ ('*re*)		

negative		
I a*m not* ('*m not*)		
you *are not* ⁶ (_____)		
he / she / it ⁷ _____ (*isn't*)	going to	play.
we *are not* ⁸ (_____)		
you ⁹ _____ (*aren't*)		
they *are not* ¹⁰ _____		

② Look at the pictures below and write what these people are going to do using these verbs.

play	rent	buy

1 Ken is
   _____*going to play*_____
   the guitar.

2 They
   _____
   tickets for the
   concert.

3 He
   _____
   a DVD.

③ Complete the table.

question				short answers
Am	I			Yes, you *are*. No, you *aren't*.
Are	you			Yes, I *am*. No, I ¹_____ .
² _____	he / she / it	going to	play?	Yes, he / she / it *is*. No, he / she / it *isn't*.
Are	we			Yes, we ³ _____ . No, we ⁴ _____ .
⁵ _____	you			Yes, you *are*. No, you *aren't*.
Are	they			Yes, they ⁶ _____ . No, they *aren't*.

④ Complete the dialogue with *going to* and the correct form of the verbs.

Nigel What ___*are you going to do*___ (you / do) with all these Amy Winehouse CDs?

Pattie I ¹_____ (learn) all her songs by heart.

Nigel Really?

Pattie Sure. I ² _____ (become) a great singer like Amy.

Nigel Wow! ³ _____ (you / take) singing lessons?

Pattie No, I ⁴ _____ . That's very expensive. I ⁵ _____ (teach) myself.

Nigel Good luck, then!

Pattie Thanks, I need it. I ⁶ _____ (work) really hard.

Nigel Great!

Pattie OK, then. I have to go. I ⁷ _____ (practise) a few songs at home.

Nigel Bye.

Need help? Go to page 57!

The present continuous (to express the future)

affirmative				negative			
I	am ('m)			I	am not ('m not)		
you	are ('re)			you	are not (aren't)		
he / she / it	is ('s)	playing		he / she / it	is not ('s)	playing	
we	are ('re)			we	are not (aren't)		
you	are ('re)			you	are not (aren't)		
they	are ('re)			they	are not (aren't)		

question			short answers
Am	I		Yes, you are. / No, you aren't
Are	you		Yes, I am. / No, I'm not.
Is	he / she / it	playing?	Yes, he / she / it is. / No, he / she / it isn't.
Are	we		Yes, we are. / No, we aren't.
Are	you		Yes, we are. / No, we aren't.
Are	they		Yes, they are. / No, they aren't.

5 What arrangements does Steven have this week? Write questions. Use the prompts and short answers and the information in Steven's diary.

1 dentist / Tuesday?

Is Steven going to the dentist on Tuesday?

No, he isn't. He's going to the dentist on Monday.

2 Francesca / at 5.00 pm on Tuesday?

_____

_____

3 karate lesson / Friday?

_____

_____

4 dinner at Grandma's / Thursday?

_____

_____

5 tennis / from 4 to 5 on Friday/

_____

_____

6 pizza at Mario's / Saturday/

_____

_____

Sunday

Monday
11.30 a.m.
dentist

Tuesday
5.00 p.m.
meet Francesca

Wednesday
10.00–12.00 a.m.
karate lesson

Thursday
12.30 p.m.
lunch at Grandma's

Friday
4.00–5.00 p.m.
tennis

Saturday
7.30 p.m.
pizza at Mario's

Functions

Giving directions

① Listen and read

Kelly	Hey, guys. I'm really sorry but I have some bad news.
Laura	What is it?
Kelly	I'm afraid I have to cancel the party. My mum's ill and she is going into hospital on Friday. I apologise but I can't do anything about it.

② Comprehension

Read the dialogue and answer the questions.

1 What is Kelly's problem?

_____

2 What does she ask Laura and Mark to help her do?

_____

3 How does Mark offer to help?

_____

4 How many people are coming to the party?

_____

③ Read and find

Read the dialogue again and write the expressions used to apologise.

_____

_____

_____

_____

Laura	Oh dear. That's terrible, Kelly. It doesn't matter about the party. Can we do anything?
Kelly	Well, can you call everybody and tell them what happened?
Mark	Sorry to interrupt, but don't do anything yet. Perhaps we can have it at my house.
Laura	But your parents are busy on Saturday, remember?
Mark	I know, but 20 people are coming to our party. I'm going to try. Don't worry.
Kelly	Thanks, Mark.

④ Write

Complete the short dialogues below. Use the expressions in the boxes to help you.

> **Apologising:**
> I'm really/so/very sorry … /
> I apologise but …

> **Accepting apologies:**
> Don't worry. / No problem. / It doesn't matter. / It's not a problem. / It's OK.

1 You forgot to buy your friend a birthday present.
You: *I'm really sorry, but I forgot to buy you a present.*
Your friend: _____

2 You dropped a bottle of milk on the floor.
You: _____
_____
Your mum: _____

3 You were too busy to visit your grandma yesterday.
You: _____
_____
Grandma: _____

Skills

① Read

Read the article and answer the questions below.

Elton John once had a hit song which said Sorry seems to be the hardest word. Why is it often difficult to say 'sorry' to other people? Well, it depends on the situation. If you bump into someone on the street by accident, then it's usually not very important or serious and it's easy to say 'sorry'. But if you do something more serious, then it's harder. If you are playing with a ball in the house and you break a vase, then it's more difficult to apologise.

Perhaps the most difficult time to say 'sorry' is when you hurt somebody's feelings ... if you make your friend cry by saying something or doing something horrible to them, for example. But it's the sign of how mature you are to go up to them and apologise and try to become friends again.

WORD LIST

bump into	_____
vase	_____
hurt somebody's feelings	_____

② Listen and answer

Listen to the dialogue these sentences are true (T) or false (F). Correct the false sentences.

1 Philip and Sandra are planning to go away for a weekend to Italy. _____

   _____

2 Sandra apologises to Philip because she can't go. _____

   _____

3 Philip's mother broke her leg yesterday.

   _____

4 Philip's parents have a shop. _____

   _____

5 Sandra is angry because Philip can't go to Rome with her. _____

   _____

③ Write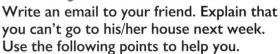

Write an email to your friend. Explain that you can't go to his/her house next week. Use the following points to help you.

✓ Apologise to him/her.

✓ Explain why you can't go.

✓ Suggest another time when you can see him/her.

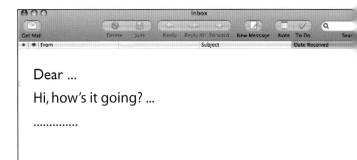

Dear ...

Hi, how's it going? ...

....

The Sahara Desert

Complete the conversation with the words in the box.

mint tea	camel	photos	desert
sand	tent	white	

A   I'm going to the Sahara Desert with my family. It is the biggest
¹ _____ in the world!

B   Are you? Wow! When are you going?

A   We are going in September and we are staying for six days. It is going to be very hot!

B   Yes, it is the hottest place on earth and there is very little water. What are you going to do?

A   We're going to ride on a ² _____ .

B   That's fantastic!

A   And we're going to meet some Bedouin people. Some of them still live in the desert. My mum says that we are going to drink some
³ _____ in their ⁴ _____ . They are going to give the tea to us.

B   Mmm. Are you going to see an oasis?

A   Yes we are going to camp at Farafra oasis. Sometimes Egyptian children also go camping there with their schools. The sand is ⁵ _____ there!

B   Are you going to take your camera?

A   Yes, there are going to be some ⁶ _____ dunes and they are very beautiful. I am going to take some ⁷ _____ It is very exciting.

B   Have a lovely time!

A   Thanks!

WORD LIST

fly	_____
ride	_____
mint	_____
sand dune	_____

② Comprehension

Read the text on page 50 again and fill in the facts about the holiday.

Holiday to the Sahara

Month _____

Number of days _____

Activities _____

_____

_____

③ Write

Write a postcard about a holiday that you enjoyed.

WOW!

The Sahara is the biggest desert in the world and covers a third of the African continent.

CRACK THE CODE

④ **Which animal names can you find below in the word snake? Circle them and then say which animal doesn't live in the desert.**

desertfoxsandcatcamelpolarbearelephantlizard

Dessert animals _____ _____ _____

_____ _____

_____ isn't a desert animal

Grammar reference

Grammar Unit 1

① Verbs followed by the *-ing* form

affirmative	negative	question	short answer
I love swimming.	I don't like dancing.	Do you like cooking?	Yes, I do. / No, I don't.
He hates studying.	He doesn't mind walking.	Does he enjoy reading?	Yes, he does. / No, he doesn't.

▶ We usually follow verbs like *love*, *like*, *enjoy*, *don't mind*, *don't like*, *hate* with the *-ing* form of the verb.

I like playing volleyball.
We love dancing.
He enjoys going fi shing.
She hates doing exercise.
I don't mind watching TV.
They don't like studying.

② Comparatives and superlatives

	adjective	comparative	superlative
Short adjectives	tall	taller	the tallest
	big	bigger	the biggest
	easy	easier	the easiest
	nice	nicer	the nicest
Long adjectives	expensive	more expensive	the most expensive
	difficult	more difficult	the most difficult
	boring	more boring	the most boring
Irregular adjectives	good	better	the best
	bad	worse	the worst
	fun	more fun	the most fun

▶ Regular comparatives and superlatives have two forms:
- When the adjective is made up of one syllable, or two syllables with a *-y* ending, we add *-er* to the comparative and *-est* to the superlative.
- When the adjective is made up of two or more syllables, we put *more* in front of the adjective to form the comparative and the *most* to form the superlative.

▶ When we compare two things, the comparative is followed by *than*.

▶ Some adjectives are irregular both in the comparative and superlative.

Grammar Unit 2

① The verb *be* (past simple)

affirmative	negative		question	short answer
	full	contracted		
I was	I was not	I wasn't	Was I?	Yes, you were. No, you weren't.
you were	you were not	you weren't	Were you?	Yes, I was. No, I wasn't.
he was	he was not	he wasn't	Was he?	Yes, he was. No, he wasn't.
she was	she was not	she wasn't	Was she?	Yes, she was. No, she wasn't.
it was	it was not	it wasn't	Was it?	Yes, it was. No, it wasn't.
we were	we were not	we weren't	Were we?	Yes, we were. No, we weren't.
you were	you were not	you weren't	Were you?	Yes, you were. No, you weren't.
they were	they were not	they weren't	Were they?	Yes, they were. No, they weren't.

▶ *be* is an irregular verb. The past simple of *be* is *was* for the first and third person singular and *were* for all the others.

▶ We form questions by inverting the subject and the verb.

▶ We form negatives with *was* and *were* followed by not (*wasn't / weren't*).

② The verb *have* (past simple)

affirmative		negative	
I / you / he / she / it / we / you / they	had	I / you / he / she / it / we / you / they	did not have (didn't have)

question			short answer	
Did	I / you / he / she / it / we / you / they	have?	Yes, I / you / he / she / it / we / you / they	did.

▶ *Have* is an irregular verb. The past simple is *had* for all persons.

▶ We form questions and negatives with *did / didn't* plus the base form of the verb.

Grammar reference

Grammar Unit 3

① The past simple (regular verbs)

affirmative	negative full	contracted
I washed	I did not wash	I didn't wash
you washed	you did not wash	you didn't wash
he washed	he did not wash	he didn't wash
she washed	she did not wash	she didn't wash
it washed	it did not wash	it didn't wash
we washed	we did not wash	we didn't wash
you washed	you did not wash	you didn't wash
they washed	they did not wash	they didn't wash

question	short answer
Did I wash?	Yes, you did. / No, you didn't.
Did you wash?	Yes, I did. / No, I didn't.
Did he wash?	Yes, he did. / No, he didn't.
Did she wash?	Yes, she did. / No, she didn't.
Did it wash?	Yes, it did. / No, it didn't.
Did we wash?	Yes, we did. / No, we didn't.
Did you wash?	Yes, you did. / No, you didn't.
Did they wash?	Yes, they did. / No, they didn't.

▶ We use the past simple to describe an action that has finished in the past.

▶ We form the past simple of regular verbs by adding -ed to the verb.

▶ We form questions with did + subject + the verb.

▶ We form questions with did not (= didn't) + the verb.

▶ We often use the past simple with expressions of time such as yesterday / last night / week / month / year … or with a date.

Grammar Unit 4

① The past simple (irregular verbs)

affirmative	negative	question	short answer
I gave	I did not (didn't) give	Did I give?	Yes, you did. / No, you didn't.
you gave	you did not (didn't) give	Did you give?	Yes, I did. / No, I didn't.
he gave	he did not (didn't) give	Did he give?	Yes, he did. / No, he didn't.
she gave	she did not (didn't) give	Did she give?	Yes, she did. / No, she didn't.
it gave	it did not (didn't) give	Did it give?	Yes, it did. / No, it didn't.
we gave	we did not (didn't) give	Did we give?	Yes, we did. / No, we didn't.
you gave	you did not (didn't) give	Did you give?	Yes, you did. / No, you didn't.
they gave	they did not (didn't) give	Did they give?	Yes, they did. / No, they didn't.

bare infinitive	past simple	bare infinitive	past simple	bare infinitive	past simple
begin	**began**	know	**knew**	say	**said**
buy	**bought**	learn	**learnt**	sing	**sang**
come	**came**	leave	**left**	see	**saw**
do	**did**	lose	**lost**	sleep	**slept**
drink	**drank**	make	**made**	speak	**spoke**
eat	**ate**	pay	**paid**	take	**took**
fall	**fell**	put	**put**	tell	**told**
find	**found**	read	**read**	think	**thought**
get	**got**	ride	**rode**	win	**won**
go	**went**	run	**ran**	write	**wrote**

▶ Irregular verbs have their own form in the past simple.

▶ As with regular verbs, we form questions and negatives with *did / didn't* + bare infinitive of the verb.

② Wh- questions

question	did	subject	verb	(additional)
What		you	do	yesterday?
Where	did	she	go?	
When		they	leave?	

▶ In a question, we put *wh-* question words at the beginning.

Grammar reference

Grammar Unit 5

 Must / mustn't

affirmative	negative	
	full	contracted
I must	I must not	I mustn't
you must	you must not	you mustn't
he must	he must not	he mustn't
she must	she must not	she mustn't
it must	it must not	it mustn't
we must	we must not	we mustn't
you must	you must not	you mustn't
they must	they must not	they mustn't

▶ We use *must* to express obligation.

▶ We follow *must* with the bare infinitive of the verb (the infinitive without *to*).

▶ In the third person singular, we don't add *-s*.

▶ We use *mustn't* to express prohibition.

▶ We rarely use questions with *must / mustn't*.

affirmative	negative	question	short answer
I have to	I do not (don't) have to	Do I have to?	Yes, you do. / No, you don't.
you have to	you do not (don't) have to	Do you have to?	Yes, I do. / No, I don't.
he has to	he does not (doesn't) have to	Does he have to?	Yes, he does. / No, he doesn't.
she has to	she does not (doesn't) have to	Does she have to?	Yes, she does. / No, she doesn't.
it has to	it does not (doesn't) have to	Does it have to?	Yes, it does. / No, it doesn't.
we have to	we do not (don't) have to	Do we have to?	Yes, we do. / No, we don't.
you have to	you do not (don't) have to	Do you have to?	Yes, you do. / No, you don't.
they have to	they do not (don't) have to	Do they have to?	Yes, they do. / No, they don't

▶ We use *have* or *has* + *to* + the bare infinitive of the verb to express obligation.

▶ The negative form *don't / doesn't have to* signifies absence of obligation, not prohibition.

▶ We form negatives with the auxiliaries *do / does*.

Grammar Unit 6

① The future with *going to*

affirmative	negative
I'm going to play	I'm not going to take
you're going to eat	you aren't going to clean
he's going to study	he isn't going to pay
she's going to visit	she isn't going to write
it's going to have	it isn't going to have
we're going to come	we aren't going to watch
you're going to speak	you aren't going to listen
they're going to swim	they aren't going to wash

question	short answer
Am I going to drink?	Yes, you are. / No, you aren't.
Are you going to come?	Yes, I am. / No, I'm not.
Is he going to speak?	Yes, he is. / No, he isn't.
Is she going to buy?	Yes, she is. / No, she isn't.
Is it going to eat?	Yes, it is. / No, it isn't.
Are we going to wait?	Yes, we are. / No, we aren't.
Are you going to play?	Yes, you are. / No, you aren't.
Are they going to sleep?	Yes, they are. / No, they aren't.

▶ One way of expressing the future is with the verb *be* + *going to* + the bare infinitive of the verb.

▶ The future with *going to* expresses a plan to do or not do something.

② The present continuous (to express the future)

affirmative	negative
I'm playing tennis this afternoon.	She isn't coming tomorrow.
We're visiting Paris next week.	They aren't sleeping at home tonight.

question	short answer
Are you coming to the party later?	Yes, I am. / No, I'm not.
Is Peter driving us home later?	Yes, he is. / No, he isn't.

▶ The future with the present continuous is used to talk about definite plans in the future.

▶ We often use it with an expression of time such as *today, tonight, this afternoon / weekend / summer* or with a date.

Word list

Unit 1

aspirin /ˈæspɪrɪn/

baker /ˈbeɪkə/

bread /bred/

butcher /ˈbʊtʃə/

cake /keɪk/

canyon /ˈkænjən/

change (n) /tʃeɪndʒ/

cheap /tʃiːp/

chemist /ˈkemɪst/

chicken /ˈtʃɪkɪn/

computer game /kəmˈpjuːtə geɪm/

continent /ˈkɒntɪnənt/

expensive /ɪkˈspensɪv/

far /fɑː/

flight /flaɪt/

florist /ˈflɒrɪst/

flower /flaʊə/

fun /fʌn/

greengrocer /ˈgriːnˌgrəʊsə/

height /haɪt/

mountain /ˈmaʊntɪn/

newsagent's /ˈnjuːzeɪdʒənts/

newspaper /ˈnjuːzpeɪpə/

ocean /ˈəʊʃən/

river /ˈrɪvə/

sausage /ˈsɒsɪdʒ/

school mark /skuːl mɑːk/

sprint record /sprɪnt ˈrekɔːd/

swimming record /ˈswɪmɪŋ ˈrekɔːd/

together /təˈgeðə/

toothbrush /ˈtuːuːθbrʌʃ/

trainers /ˈtreɪnəz/

travel agent /ˈtrævəl ˈeɪdʒənt/

TV guide /ˌtiːˈviː gaɪd/

valley /ˈvæli/

waterfall /ˈwɔːtəfɔːl/

weight /weɪt/

Unit 2

active /ˈæktɪv/

actor /ˈæktə/

aeroplane /ˈeərəpleɪn/

angry /ˈæŋgri/

bicycle /ˈbaɪsɪkəl/

boat /bəʊt/

bored /bɔːd/

bus /bʌs/

car /kɑː/

chance /tʃɑːns/

close to /kləʊs tuː/

cup of tea /kʌp əv tiː/

dangerous /ˈdeɪndʒərəs/

daughter /ˈdɔːtə/

excited /ɪkˈsaɪtɪd/

have a bad time /hæv ə bæd taɪm/

huge /hjuːdʒ/

job /dʒɒb/

late /leɪt/

lovely /ˈlʌvli/

money /ˈmʌni/

motorbike /ˈməʊtəbaɪk/

music system /'mjuːzɪk 'sɪstəm/

office /'ɒfɪs/

on foot /ɒn fʊt/

passenger /'pæsɪndʒə/

passion /'pæʃən/

photographer /fə'tɒgrəfə/

plane /pleɪn/

present (n) /'prezənt/

scooter /'skuːtə/

simple /'sɪmpəl/

singer /'sɪŋə/

son /sʌn/

station /'steɪʃən/

successful /sək'sesfʊl/

sunny /'sʌni/

ticket /'tɪkɪt/

transport /'trænspɔːt/

tricycle /'traɪsɪkəl/

tube /tjuːb/

train /treɪn/

warm /wɔːm/

weather /'weðə/

Unit 3

amazing /ə'meɪzɪŋ/

angel /'eɪndʒəl/

birthday party /'bɜːθdeɪ 'pɑːti/

candle /'kændəl/

carriage /'kærɪdʒ/

Christmas /'krɪsməs/

coach /kəʊtʃ/

costume /'kɒstjuːm/

delicious /dɪ'lɪʃəs/

design (v) /dɪ'zaɪn/

exclamation /ɪksləˈmeɪʃən/

fairy /'feəri/

famous sights /'feɪməs saɪts/

fancy dress party /'fænsi dres 'pɑːti/

ghost /gəʊst/

high /haɪ/

horse /hɔːs/

in the country /ɪn ðə 'kʌntri/

it's about …/ɪts ə'baʊt/

journey /'dʒɜːni/

lake /leɪk/

large /lɑːdʒ/

meet (v) /miːt/

midday /ˌmɪd'deɪ/

midnight /'mɪdnaɪt/

New Year /ˌnjuː 'jɪə/

people /'piːpəl/

pirate /'paɪrət/

pool party /puːl 'pɑːti/

princess /ˌprɪn'ses/

pyjamas /pɪ'dʒɑːməz/

ready /'redi/

sleepover /'sliːpəʊvə/

surprise party /sə'praɪz 'pɑːti/

swimming costume /'swɪmɪŋ 'kɒstjuːm/

tired /'taɪəd/

tree /triː/

wedding /'wedɪŋ/

witch /wɪtʃ/

young /jʌŋ/

Word list

Unit 4

action /ˈækʃən/

alien /ˈeɪliən/

archaeologist /aːkiˈɒlədʒɪst/

astronaut /ˈæstrənɔːt/

attractive /əˈtræktɪv/

beef /biːf/

boring /ˈbɔːrɪŋ/

bracelet /ˈbreɪslɪt/

Caribbean /ˌkærɪˈbiən/

character /ˈkærɪktə/

chemistry /ˈkemɪstri/

clothes /kləʊðz/

comedy /ˈkɒmədi/

detective /dɪˈtektɪv/

dinner /ˈdɪnə/

evil /ˈiːvəl/

excellent /ˈeksələnt/

explosion /ɪkˈspləʊʒən/

full of /fʊl əv/

funny /ˈfʌni/

get married /get ˈmærid/

gold /gəʊld/

historical /hɪˈstɒrɪkəl/

horror /ˈhɒrə/

jacket /ˈdʒækɪt/

king /kɪŋ/

lamb /læm/

laugh (v) /laːf/

leader /ˈliːdə/

motor racing /ˈməʊtə ˈreɪsɪŋ/

musical /ˈmjuːzɪkəl/

mummy /ˈmʌmi/

oil /ɔɪl/

packet /ˈpækɪt/

papyrus /ˈpæpɪrəs/

past /paːst/

pelican /ˈpelɪkən/

pharaoh /ˈfeərəʊ/

picture /ˈpɪktʃə/

pocket /ˈpɒkɪt/

prince /prɪns/

prison /ˈprɪzən/

pyramid /ˈpɪrəmɪd/

queen /kwiːn/

romance /ˈrəʊmæns/

save (v) /seɪv/

science fiction /ˈsaɪəns ˈfɪkʃən/

sesame /ˈsesəmi/

space /speɪs/

space ship /ˈspeɪs ˌʃɪp/

subject /ˈsʌbdʒɪkt/

sunglasses /ˈsʌglaːsɪz/

theme /θiːm/

thriller /ˈθrɪlə/

tomb /tuːm/

Unit 5

Arctic /ˈaːktɪk/

angry /ˈæŋgri/

Antarctic /ˈænˈtaːktɪk/

bank /bæŋk/

behind /bɪˈhaɪnd/

bins /bɪnz/

café /ˈkæfeɪ/

check (v) /tʃek/

church /tʃɜːtʃ/

cinema /ˈsɪnɪmaː/

credit card /ˈkredɪt kaːd/

crossroads /ˈkrɒsrəʊdz/

department store /dɪˈpaːtmənt stɔː/

dirty /ˈdɜːti/

garage /ˈgæraːʒ/

go past /gəʊ paːst/

go straight on /gəʊ streɪt ɒn/

hospital /ˈhɒspɪtəl/

ice /aɪs/

ill /ɪl/

library /ˈlaɪbrəri/

loud /laʊd/

museum /mjuːˈziːəm/

near /nɪə/

need (v) /niːd/

next to /nekst tuː/

on the corner /ɒn ðə ˈkɔːnə/

opposite /ˈɒpəzɪt/

optional /ˈɒpʃənəl/

pavements /ˈpeɪvmənts/

police station /pəˈliːs ˈsteɪʃən/

post office /pəʊst ˈɒfɪs/

printer /ˈprɪntə/

quiet /ˈkwaɪət/

side /saɪd/

stamp /stæmp/

supermarket /ˈsuːpəmaːkɪt/

town hall /taʊn haːl/

trip /trɪp/

wallet /ˈwɒlɪt/

Unit 6

bass guitar /beɪs gɪˈtaː/

by accident /baɪ ˈæksɪdənt/

by heart /baɪ haːt/

camel /ˈkæməl/

clarinet /ˌklærɪˈnet/

classical music /ˈklæsɪkəl ˈmjuːzɪk/

cry /kraɪ/

dentist /ˈdentɪst/

desert /ˈdezət/

disco /ˈdɪskəʊ/

drums /drʌmz/

folk /fəʊk/

fox /fɒks/

guitar /gɪˈtaː/

interrupt /ˌɪntəˈrʌpt/

keyboard /ˈkiːbɔːd/

lead guitar /liːd gɪˈtaː/

lead singer /liːd ˈsɪŋə/

lizard /ˈlɪzəd/

mature /məˈtjʊə/

organ /ˈɔːgən/

piano /piˈænəʊ/

pop music /pɒp ˈmjuːzɪk/

sand /sænd/

saxophone /ˈsæksəfəʊn/

singer /ˈsɪŋə/

soul /səʊl/

techno /ˈteknəʊ/

tent /tent/

trombone /trɒmˈbəʊn/

trumpet /ˈtrʌmpɪt/

vase /vaːz/

violin /ˌvaɪəˈlɪn/

Exit test

Name _____ Surname _____ Class _____ Date _____

① Match the shops and the products you can buy there.

e.g. newsagent's – magazine

1	baker's	a	a kilo of pears
2	butcher's	b	roses
3	florist's	c	a kilo of pork
4	greengrocer's	d	a loaf of bread

1 _____ 2 _____ 3 _____ 4 _____

② Write the comparatives and superlatives of the adjectives.

Adjective	Comparative	Superlative
e.g. small	smaller	smallest
1 big	_____	_____
2 nice	_____	_____
3 pretty	_____	_____
4 good	_____	_____

③ Unscramble the words to form methods of transport.

e.g. rtma tram

1 rac _____ 5 ctosore _____
2 atirn _____ 6 toba _____
3 usb _____ 7 kibe _____
4 ixat _____ 8 no tofo _____

④ Complete the sentences with the correct past simple form of the verb be or have.

e.g. I was with my friends yesterday.

1 We _____ at the cinema last night.

2 When _____ she _____ her exam?

3 _____ you pleased with your presents?

4 She _____ any friends to play with.

⑤ Write the past simple of the regular verbs.

e.g. walk   walked

1 plan _____ 5 marry _____
2 decide _____ 6 travel _____
3 try _____ 7 work _____
4 paint _____ 8 stop _____

⑥ Write sentences to perform the functions.

e.g. Suggest that you go to the cinema.

Let's go to the cinema

1 Suggest you go to the seaside next Saturday.

Why _____?

2 Refuse the suggestion – you're visiting your grandparents.

I'm _____?

3 Invite your friend to watch a DVD with you after school.

_____?

4 Refuse the invitation. You have to do your homework

_____

7 Complete the sentences with the past simple of the irregular verbs.

e.g. I made a birthday cake for my mum last weekend. (make)

1 I _____ two James Bond films on Saturday. (see)

2 We _____ pasta in Milan. (eat)

3 My mother _____ a new coat. (buy)

4 He _____ that his answer was wrong. (know)

8 Complete the sentences with the past simple of the irregular verbs.

(+ = affirmative; – = negative; ? = question)

e.g. I broke my mum's best vase yesterday. (break +)

1 Paul _____ his scooter too fast in the city centre. (drive +)

2 I _____ my friends last night. (meet –)

3 _____ your mum _____ her old car? (sell ?)

4 They _____ us to the match yesterday. (take –)

9 Match the places in the town with things you can do there.

e.g. cinema – you watch films.

1	school	a	you take out money
2	hotel	b	you buy food
3	supermarket	c	you learn
4	bank	d	you sleep

1 _____ 2 _____ 3 _____ 4 _____

10 Complete the sentences with the correct form of the verb.

(+ = affirmative; – = negative; ? = interrogative)

e.g. I must buy a present for my mum's birthday. (must +)

1 You _____ run inside the school buildings. (must –)

2 _____ I _____ finish my homework before dinner? (have to ?)

3 They _____ try to work harder before the exams. (must +)

4 You _____ go to school tomorrow. It's a holiday. (have to –)

11 Identify the sentences as present continuous as future (PCF), the *going to* future (GTF) or the present continuous for now (PCN).

e.g. I'm living in Milan at the moment. PCN

1 I'm going to France next summer. _____

2 He's going to visit his cousins next weekend. _____

3 They're sitting down quietly now. _____

4 We're playing an important match tomorrow. _____

Total: _____ / 44

HEINLE
CENGAGE Learning

Holiday Explorer 2
David A. Hill

Publisher: Jason Mann

Adaptations Manager: Alistair Baxter

Assistant Editor: Manuela Barros

Senior Marketing Manager: Ruth McAleavey

Senior Content Project Editor: Natalie Griffith

Senior Production Controller: Paul Herbert

National Geographic Liaison: Leila Hishmeh

Art Director: Natasa Arsenidou

Cover Designer: Nora Spiliopoulou

Text Designer: Sofia Fourtouni

Audio: EFS Television Production Ltd

Acknowledgements

The publisher gratefully acknowledges the editorial contribution of Lisa Darrand.

The publisher would also like to thank Bethan Williams for her invaluable contribution.

ISBN: 978-1-111-39879-8

Heinle, Cengage Learning EMEA
Cheriton House
North Way
Andover
Hampshire
SP10 5BE
United Kingdom

Cengage Learning is a leading provider of customised learning solutions with office locations around the globe, including Singapore, the United Kingdom, Australia, Mexico, Brazil and Japan. Locate our local office at:
international.cengage.com/region

Cengage Learning products are represented in Canada by Nelson Education, Ltd.

Visit Heinle online at **elt.heinle.com**
Visit our corporate website at **cengage.com**

Photo credits

The publishers would like to thank the following sources for permission to reproduce their copyright protected photographs:

Cover photo: (David Edwards / National Geographic Image Collection)

pp 2 (Tim Fitzharris/Minden Pictures/National Geographic Image Collection), (Carsten Peter/ National Geographic Image Collection), (James P. Blair/National Geographic Image Collection), (Gerry Ellis/Minden Pictures/National Geographic Image Collection), (Alaska Stock Images/National Geographic Image Collection), (Gerry Ellis/ Minden Pictures/National Geographic Image Collection), 3 (Shutterstock.com), 4 (Shutterstock.com), 5 (Shutterstock.com), 7 (Shutterstock.com), 8 (Shutterstock.com), 9 (Shutterstock.com), 10 (Tim Fitzharris/Minden Pictures/National Geographic Image Collection), 12 (Shutterstock.com), 13 (Shutterstock.com), 15 (Shutterstock.com), 16 (Shutterstock.com), 17 (Pictorial Press Ltd/Alamy), 18 (Carsten Peter/ National Geographic Image Collection), 19 (Shutterstock.com), 20 (Shutterstock.com), 21 (Shutterstock.com), 23 (Shutterstock.com), 24 (Shutterstock.com), 25 (Alfio Ferlito/Fotolia), 26 (James P. Blair/National Geographic Image Collection), 27 (Shutterstock.com), 28 (Shutterstock.com), 29 (Shutterstock.com), 31 (Shutterstock.com), 32 (Shutterstock.com), 33 (Shutterstock.com), 34 (Gerry Ellis/Minden Pictures/National Geographic Image Collection), 34 [inset (Kenneth Garrett/National Geographic Image Collection)], 34 (Lukiyanova Natalia/Frenta/Shutterstock), 34 [inset (Gerry Ellis/Minden Pictures/National Geographic Image Collection)], 34 [inset (Kenneth Garrett/National Geographic Image Collection)], 34 [inset (Sean Sexton Collection/ Corbis)], 35 (Shutterstock.com), 35 (Dreamstime), 36 (Shutterstock.com), 37 (Shutterstock.com), 39 (Shutterstock.com), 40 (Shutterstock.com), 41(RLP Stock Photo/ Alamy), 41 (Shutterstock.com), 41 (Shutterstock.com), 42 (Alaska Stock Images/National Geographic Image Collection), 43 (Ekaterina Starshaya/Istockphoto), 43 (Shutterstock.com), 44 (Shutterstock.com), 45 (Shutterstock.com), 48 (Shutterstock.com), 49 (Shutterstock.com), 50 (Gerry Ellis/Minden Pictures/National Geographic Image Collection), 50 [inset (Abraham Nowitz/National Geographic Image Collection)], 50 [inset (Gordan Gahan/National Geographic Image Collection)], 50 [inset (Michael Poliza/National Geographic Image Collection)], 50 [inset (Carsten Peter/National Geographic Image Collection)], 50 [inset (Bobby Model/National Geographic Image Collection)], 51 [left to right (Shutterstock.com), (Nico Smit/Istockphoto), (James Richey/Istockphoto), (Bigstockphoto), (Dreamstime),

Illustrations by Katerina Chrysochloou

Printed by Seng Lee Press, Singapore
2 3 4 5 6 7 8 9 10 – 14 13 12 11 10